Kali's Songs
and other poems

North Wall
Publishing

Kali's Songs: a collection of poems written by Peter Mullins. Illustrated by Emily Connor. Book design and layout by Victoria Hydes. Content © Peter Mullins and Emily Connor 2014. Kali's Songs is a North Wall publication in association with CPO Media. All Rights Reserved. No part of this publication may be reproduced or transmitted in any form or by any means, electronic or mechanical, including photocopying, recording or any information storage or retrieval systems without prior permission.

ISBN: 978-0-9568175-4-9

CPO Media www.mycpomedia.com

Contents

Kali's Songs

Let loose at last   2
A cairn in a cave   4
Delight with me   6
The shipwreck   8
Asa is pleading   10
Einar set to lure me in   12
A fisherman scorned   14
Ode on a wall hanging   16
Remembering Ermingard   18

Orpheus and Eurydice

Orpheus and Eurydice   22

Divine Poems

A Winter Burial   26
Caught Out   28
Hide and Seek   30
Mary of the Cross   32
Pointing   34
A Metheringham Tsunami   36
That we might see the stars   38
From a Malmesbury Sequence   40
Matinlight   42

Notes   44

Kali's songs

versions of nine of
Rognvald jarl Kali Kolsson's
poems from the
Orkneyinga Saga

2

Let loose at last

We'd wasted five weeks waiting,
      our feet festering in filth,
mired in mud in the middle
      of Grimsby, grimly grounded.

Now, let loose, we laugh aloud
      on the gulls' moor's mounds, mounted
on elk-back, bounding breakers,
      our bow's beak set on Bergen.

4

A cairn in a cave

We pile up stones to mask our fear
     and keep the cave's strong ghouls away
who in the deep of Doll's dark hole
     maintain their grip on rings of gold.

We pile up stones to mark our feat:
     perhaps some men will skim the sea
and then on this our awful route
     will find our cairn already built.

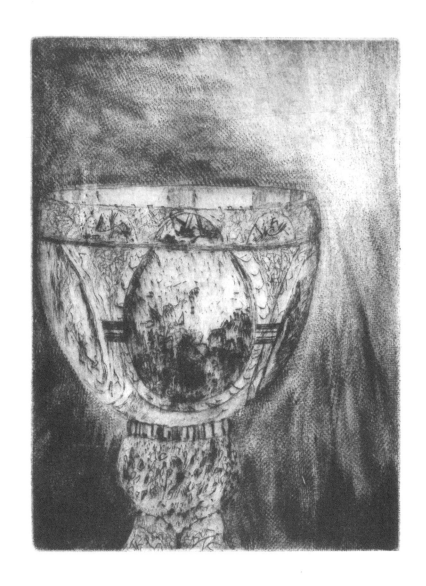

Delight with me

Hands which swung felled-trees through water
stroke the gold that snakes in loops
     where the hunter's hawk last rested,
stroke the gold once executed
     by such hammer wielding hands.

Drink with me, great God of all fate,
sing of one tree-tall-slender
     sing of her bright treasure-bearing,
delight me with at all her splendour,
     sing and to her beauty drink.

8

The shipwreck

In widowing weather, a wave
    hit *Help* hard and shot *Arrow* down.
Remember it now: how the brave,
    while soaking, let nobody drown.

Asa is pleading

Storm soaked and freezing,
Asa is pleading
      with teeth chat-at-atering
      and speech stut-ut-utering
for space by the fire
to get herself warm.

12

Einar set to lure me in

In my speech the storm surge sings
     of Einar set to lure me in
at whose farm the forge fire flames
     with burning swords and twisting claims.

A fisherman scorned

She, silky and soft, scorns my smock
and laughs a lot longer than I like
at me, reeking and rough, rolling
where I stumbled on the slipway's slope.

Few fathom this fisherman's fame
or have a hunch how I hauled heavy
beams and boats bravely behind me
up this slope sure-footed at sunrise.

Ode on a wall hanging

Old warrior, frozen on the tapestry,
with scabbard empty, sword upraised,
an arm now swinging down,
bold warrior, never, never canst thou kill
however angry thou may'st be,
though winning near the goal.

Remembering Ermingard

Her hair flows like fire;
      our fire claims our foes.
Her wine wet our lips;
      our blades cut their throats.

Orpheus and Eurydice:

a version of
Rainer Maria Rilke's
poem

Orpheus and Eurydice

A mine-shaft opens into hell
where what seem veins of silver ore
are streaks of silent human souls
whose life drained off solidifies
and marks the roots a startling red,

where pit-props swarm between dark walls
and broken boards span gulfs and voids,
while roofs reflect the great grey pools
as if the rain would never stop.

A fractured mind pulled at a thread
and stretched it out, imagining
a gentle road through pastures green,
on which it then began to walk,
fit, smart, quiet and purposeful,
with eyes fixed firm in front of it,
with heavy hands tucked tight away,
with strides which gobbled up the path,

quite unaware how the laments
which flowered from its singing-grief
were now so grafted into it
that it was like an olive tree
smothered by a wild briar.

One shard of mind dashed on ahead,
ran fast around, looped back again,
one quivered still to catch a sense
of others who might be behind,
half thought it did, but caught no hint
above the shaking of its coat,
the panting from its charging round;
it told itself that they were there,
said it loudly, heard the words die
away into a stilling fear
that to look round would snap the thread –
the very path they walked upon –
and let the shaft re-swallow them.

There ought to be no mystery:
there ought to be a messenger,
a shining or a hooded one,
come swift as if on feet with wings,
a magic wand in his right hand
and in his left there should be – she,

she who called out more singing-grief
than any woman ever had,
a wailing-world made from mourning
with routes and contours cut by grief,
whose habitations of lament
lay under a lament-full sky
with suns, stars and constellations
sent off course by lamentations;
so greatly was she loved and sung.

But she walks alone and elsewhere,
her steps caught on her graveclothes' hem,
stumbling without irritation,
great with the hope carried in her
not of his path, not in his song,
but replete with sweet dark death-fruit,
an abundance of being dead,
an unfathomable newness -

and made innocent once again
(the bud which opened up to him
drawn tight like petals in the night,
even the touch of a God would
now be a painful intrusion).

The songs were not about her now,
her scent, her bed, who's possession:
she was the flow of long loosed hair,
the emptying of rain-full cloud,
the largesse of gift all given.

She was as firmly rooted there
as she had been in the moments
when the carer tried to stop her
with voice catching as she told her
he was standing at the exit
looking for her farewell greeting
and her reply was to say - 'Who?',
while he, unrecognised, saw her,
holding hands with the mystery,
walking away without message,
her steps caught on her graveclothes' hem,
stumbling without irritation.

Divine songs

nine further poems
from ministry
on the edge of Grimsby

A Winter Burial

'Is that a boat?'
whispered the child
as the coffin
was carried out.

'Yes, in a way'
his mother said
as the fresh thought
kindled her hope.

And the low sun
flamed over it
as it drifted
beyond her reach.

Caught Out

The rough raucous cry
     of the gull inland
swooping and riding
     a harsh grating call
is laughter when thrown
     across sea and sand.

The screech in my ears
     pounds blood as I stand
as curtains glide round
     the bier and the pall:
the rough raucous cry
     of the gull inland.

No one who stands there
     suspects I'm unmanned;
suspects what I'm too
     far in to recall
is the laughter thrown
     across sea and sand;

suspects there are things
     no soul can withstand
(abuse, blight and chance;
     traps dug for us all;
the rough raucous cry
     of the gull inland);

suspects only then
     can we understand
what seeds itself there,
     albeit so small,
brings laughter when thrown
     across sea and sand;

supects we each need
     a free empty hand
by which to be caught
     as we laugh and fall.
the rough raucous cry
     of the gull inland
is laughter when thrown
     across sea and sand.

Hide and Seek

When Mary's time
    to give birth was
she bore as son
    Almighty God,
who had himself
    this whole world wrought.

She wound him round
    in winding rags
and put him in
    the cattle trough,
without much clue
    what else to do.

He did not wish
    to hide from men
so secretly
    so wretchedly
in cattle trough
    bound up in rags.

Instead he chose
    the rags as clues
to who he was,
    to where God is,
which heaven shows
    to those who watch.

Mary of the Cross

Sweet Mary, distraught

distraught and keening,
keening at the death,
the death of her child,
her child once taunted,
taunted now herself,
herself in the place,

the place wet with blood,
with blood which now stains,
now stains her tears red,
tears red on her breast,
her breast tight with grief,
with grief like none since,

none since, Mary sweet.

34

Pointing

The blocks of ironstone
bound by rigid mortar
flake away
like some dry mud cracking
in a shallow hollow
once a pool
or honey coloured cells
in a comb of pointing
congealing.

A mix far too strong to
take the stone's expansion
and fall out
slapped in to free a man
from the tedium of
repointing,
the whole point of pointing
to take the punishment
forgotten.

Inside, with the same care,
the man places people
in a vice
insisting that the words
should be stronger than the
lives they frame
while the words' own Word waits
to take the strain of our
distortions.

A Metheringham Tsunami

When throwing prayer, it seems new waves are born,
which flow through bay window, retaining wall,
a wide expanse of leaf and twig strewn lawn,
and, with light rippling behind them, the tall
trees circling the garden; being borne
on to hints of a path where people run,
converse, walk dogs, and turn aside to mourn
where gravestones stand, to reach the setting sun.

The play of light dis-orientates, shorn
of our long grown matted habit which takes
meaning from facing east, weaving things worn
facing west: the stone moves and the earth quakes
behind us; we do not look for the dawn,
but look across the waves that moving makes.

That we might see the stars

Begin with richness in the mouth
like date-palm fruit, let sweetness speak,
let each truth, each re-telling, make

guest-ready all our shelters, each
blest with fare citrus-sharp, with air
zest-laden, word and deed made one.

If flavour's source is lost, still let
goodness be pressed, like myrtle crushed,
to anoint, to scent even those

who wander willow's watercourse,
wild waste without wisdom's whetting,
wilderness without what work wafts.

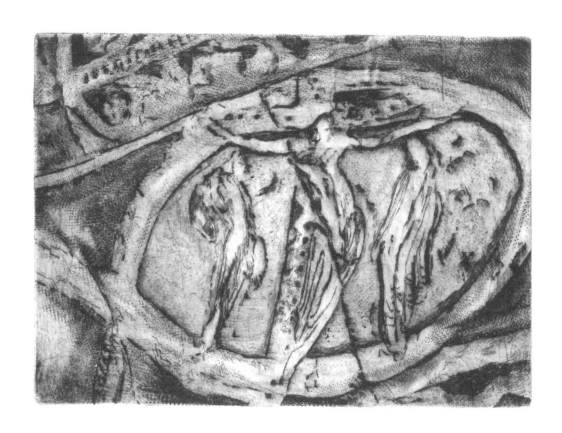

40

From a Malmesbury Sequence

Huddled there in fear,
the table before them like
the curve of the world.

Still closest to you,
echoing your body's squirm
untouched by your arms.

Bent, intent with grief,
with their delicate fingers
placing you gently.

Unexpectedly
erect, you gaze out ahead,
your banner streaming.

Matinlight

On rare days, light slants though the east window,
catches the plain north wall, and plays with it;
the leaves of an ash almost brush the glass
so dappling colour takes the breeze's lead,
pools of liquid light baptise the lime-wash,
and I find I've stopped piling on new words,
like those moments when a phrase in the Psalm
becomes unexpectedly translucent.

Notes

Kali's Songs. Kali Kolsson was a twelfth century Earl of Orkney, and a Crusader, who ruled and was canonised with the name Rognvald. Poems attributed to him run through the *Orkneyinga Saga*. His poetry consistently avoids using words like sailor, sea or ship, warrior, weapon or woman. Instead he uses what are called 'kennings', which are almost like crossword clues.

Let loose at last. Written after returning from his first teenage trading trip.   In this poem he uses 'marshes of the gull' for 'sea' (which is what Emily has illustrated) and 'elk of the prow' for 'ship'.

A cairn in a cave. Written after a teenage pot-holing adventure on an island.

Delight with me. An exhibition piece claiming to have been composed calmly as his ship sank beneath him during a great storm. Some of the kennings in the original are two layered, beginning with 'snake of the bridge of the hawk' for 'arm-ring'.

Storm soaked and freezing. Written about the survivors of the wreck; Emily pictures the view of the survivors once they have climbed to safety. The words 'at-at-ata' and 'hut-ut-uta' both appear in the original.

Einar set to lure me in. Written about a suspect offer of shelter after the wreck.

A fisherman scorned. Written having helped a fishing expedition in disguise. The first kenning in the original is 'the wise goddess of silk' for 'woman'.

Ode on a wall hanging. Written as a competition piece about the wall hanging. My version is a joke (borrowing from Keats' *Ode on a Grecian Urn* which has 'bold lover, never, never canst thou kiss though winning near the goal'); Keats would have had the same idea independently since the *Orkneyinga Saga* was not available in English during his life-time. Until this page, Emily's illustrations have been drypoint etching; this and the next illustration are two of four which she has drawn.

Remembering Ermingard. Written recalling his lover while laying siege.

Orpheus and Eurydice. This longer poem stands in the middle of this collection. Rilke's original names Hermes in the title but he has been demythologised in this version. I remember soon after my father's death an absolute conviction that he was about to walk through the door and say it had all been a misunderstanding despite the fact I knew he wouldn't. I have also spent time alongside those with mental disorder and those with relatives with dementia. These experiences were all unconsciously in the background when I developed this version of the famous German poem.

A Winter Burial. The setting was the porch of St Peter's, Great Limber, and Emily's drawing was made in this same churchyard.

Caught Out. The setting of this villanelle is the Chapel at Grimsby Crematorium. A hint which some readers have found helpful is that, in contrast to the usual use of language, and in line with the gulls, the poem assumes it is better and safer to be 'out' than 'in'.

Hide and Seek. A version of lines from the Ormulum ("& Sannte Marʒess time wass þatt ʒho þa shollde childenn…") produced at Bourne Abbey in Lincolnshire at the same time as the *Orkneyinga Saga*; this version has been set to music by David Overton and used at Carol Services at Grimsby Minster. Emily has drawn the bundle of rags within which the child is hidden.

Mary of the Cross. A version of a verse from the fourteenth century *Song of the Holy Maidens*; in the original, the beginning of each line picks up the word used at the end of the previous line.

Pointing. The setting is the tower walls at St George's, Bradley. Emily's study is of an eroded stone in the wall of that church.

A Metheringham Tsunami. The setting of this sonnet is the view from the Old Rectory's Drawing Room which is now the Community of St Francis' Chapel. Emily's tsunami is a monoprint.

That we might see the stars. The four fruits associated with the Jewish feast of Booths are sometimes taken to have taste representing the teaching of the scriptures (palm), smell representing good works (myrtle), both (citron) or neither (willow). Both the title and Emily's illustration pick up the requirement that those who live in booths during the festival must be able to see the sky.

From a Malmesbury Sequence. Verses responding to the twelfth century carvings on the Abbey's south door: Last Supper, Crucifixion (which is what Emily illustrates directly), Burial and Resurrection.

Matinlight. The setting is the chancel at St Nicolas', Great Coates, which is what Emily illustrates directly.

Peter Mullins has been a parish priest in Grimsby since 1999; he ought to be resigned to supposedly witty plays on the grimness of the town (a thirteenth century version of this 'joke' features in the first poem in this collection) but is actually glad that so much of this volume celebrates the area instead. He is Rector of Great and Little Coates with Bradley (the 'West Grimsby Team Ministry') and a Canon of Lincoln Cathedral, and he has been Rural Dean of Grimsby and Cleethorpes, the context from which most of the poems in the second half of this collection have arisen.

Emily Connor is studying for a BA (Hons) in Fine Art Practice at Grimsby University Centre where she says specialising in print has given her the opportunity to focus on particular techniques especially intaglio including collograph, drypoint and acid etchings with a developing style of mark making coupled with a manipulation of the fluidity of surface ink. Drawing has been of huge importance to her preparing work for this collection so that the prints are are extension of it - the drawing influencing her etching technique and the printmaking influencing the mark making in her drawing.

Grimsby Institute Group. Peter is an Honorary Fellow of the Grimsby Institute Group having been a Governor for a number of years. The Group's University Centre is one of the largest providers of Higher Education in the Further Education sector and only the third to be awarded Foundation Degree Awarding Powers. One of the first licences for local television has been awarded to the wider area mainly because of the quality of work in the Grimsby Institute Group's media department. Peter is therefore delighted that the Grimsby Institute Group and the University Centre contribute to this book through Emily's illustrations.

St Andrew's Hospice. Peter's links with St Andrew's Hospice are more limited, although he briefly helped cover a vacancy in the appointment of its Chaplain. It provides local adult and regional children's hospice services and is supported by an incredible number of hundreds of local volunteers. Peter is therefore delighted that St Andrew's Hospice will benefit from the proceeds of this book.

CPO Media. Peter has been involved in what was Grimsby's Community Press Office since its earliest days publishing local community magazines. He has continued as a Director of what is now CPO Media, for a number of years as its Chair. CPO Media continues to use training and publication as a regeneration tool. North Wall Publishing is CPO Media's imprint, the most successful of whose publications are *Distant Water* and *The Women They Left Behind* about the local fishing industry. Peter is therefore delighted that CPO Media and North Wall contribute to this book as its publisher.